Spiders

Rebecca Gilpin
Designed by Zöe Wray

Illustrated by Tetsuo Kushii, Zöe Wray and David Wright
Consultants: Ken Preston-Mafham and Dr. Rod Preston-Mafham
Reading consultant: Alison Kelly, Roehampton University

Contents

A close look

Spiders have eight legs. Most of them have eight eyes, but some of them can't see very well.

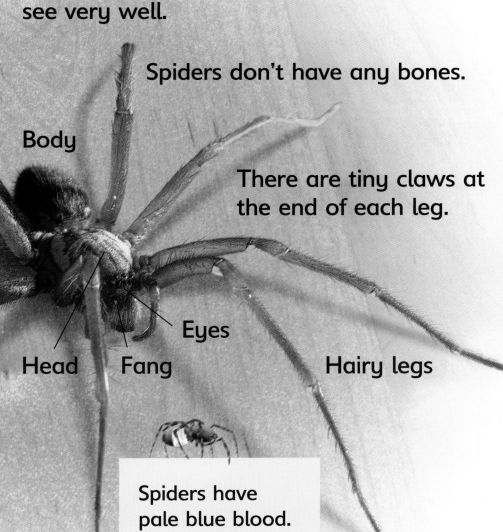

Spiders don't have any bones.

Body

There are tiny claws at the end of each leg.

Eyes

Head   Fang   Hairy legs

Spiders have pale blue blood.

A place to live

Spiders live in many different places. Most of them live outside, even where it is very hot or cold.

Many spiders live on the webs they make.

Others live in holes in the ground.

Spiders even live in deserts where it is very dry.

This lynx spider is on a cactus that grows in a desert.

4

Spiders also live in people's houses. They hide in cracks and in dark corners.

A lot of spiders live on plants.

This hairy tarantula lives in a hot, wet forest.

Spider webs

Lots of spiders make webs to catch food. Spider webs are made from silk which is made in the spider's body.

Silk

A spider makes a line of silk, which sticks onto a plant.

The spider adds lots and lots of lines of silk.

It goes around and around and adds more silk.

Webs are sticky so they can catch flies. Spiders have oily legs so they don't stick to their webs.

Try looking for webs on damp mornings. Tiny drops of water stick to them. This makes them easier to see.

Catching food

Once a spider has made a web, it waits to catch some food.

A fly flies into the web and gets stuck.

The spider runs across to the fly.

It covers the fly with silk, to keep it still.

Jumping spiders don't make webs. They sneak up on insects, then pounce on them.

This kind of spider hangs from a line of silk, holding a small web between its legs.

When an insect goes past, the spider drops down. The insect gets stuck in the web.

Sticky web

Bolas spiders use a sticky ball on the end of a line of silk to catch moths.

Eating

Spiders have sharp fangs which they use to kill the things they catch.

A spider bites a fly with its fangs. Poison shoots inside the fly.

The fly's insides turn mushy and the spider sucks them up.

Spiders eat flies and bugs. Some even eat wasps.

Most spiders eat little flies. Some can eat flies that are bigger than they are.

This spider is eating a damselfly.

Several kinds of spiders even eat small frogs!

A big surprise

Some spiders, such as trapdoor spiders, use tricks to catch food.

1. The spider digs a hole with its fangs.

2. It makes a door from soil and silk.

3. The spider hides. A beetle walks past.

4. The spider jumps out and attacks.

If a trapdoor spider catches something that it doesn't like to eat, it throws it out of its hole.

Crab spiders
walk sideways,
like crabs. They
hide in flowers so
that they can't
be seen.

When a bug
lands on the
flowers, the
spider bites it
and eats it.

Can you see the
spider hiding in
these flowers?

Living underwater

Water spiders live underwater in webs full of air. These webs are not like other webs, because they are not used to catch food.

Their webs are attached to water plants.

First, the spider makes a web under the water. Then it goes to the surface.

Then, it sticks its legs above the water and catches a big bubble of air.

The spider takes the bubble to its web and lets it go. It fills its web with lots of bubbles.

The spider catches food underwater and goes back to its web to eat.

Eggs and babies

Baby spiders hatch out of tiny spider eggs.
This is what happens before they hatch.

A mother
spider makes
a silk mat.

She lays lots
of tiny eggs
on the mat.

She covers the
eggs, to make
an egg sac.

Some spiders hide their egg sacs to
keep them safe.

This spider is
carrying her
white egg sac.

There is a tiny baby spider in each egg in the egg sac.

The spiders grow bigger. They break out of the eggs.

The baby spiders all hatch at the same time and leave the egg sac.

Baby spiders are called spiderlings.

Getting bigger

A spider's skin is not stretchy, so it gets too big for its skin, as it grows.

Silk——

1. A spider stops moving and hangs from a line of silk.

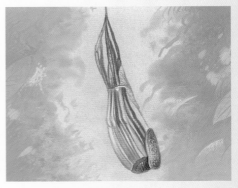

2. Its skin splits open. Underneath, there is a new stretchy skin.

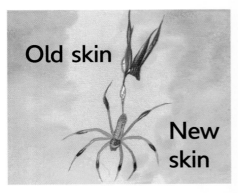

Old skin

New skin

3. The spider climbs out of its old skin. Its new skin stretches.

4. The skin hardens. The spider is bigger than it was before.

Most spiders change their skins several times as they grow.

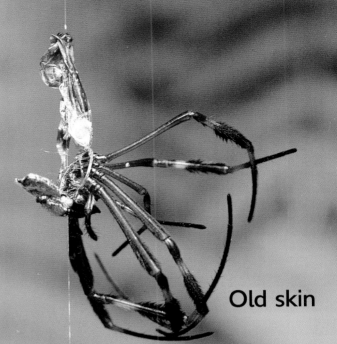

Old skin

This golden orb weaver spider is resting after climbing out of her old skin.

Her body is about as long as one of your fingers.

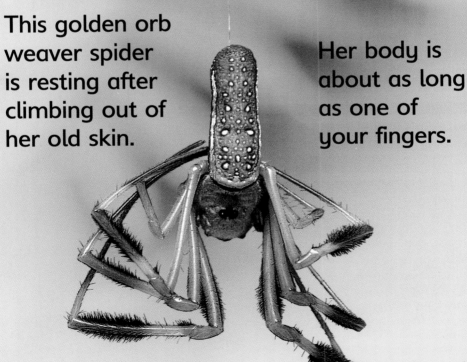

Little and large

Tarantulas are the biggest kind of spiders. Some tarantulas are so big that their legs would touch each side of a dinner plate.

This is a red-kneed tarantula.

Spitting spiders are about the same size as a pea.

They catch insects to eat by spitting sticky silk over them.

Male

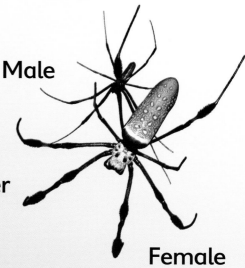

Female spiders are often bigger than males.

Female

The smallest spider in the world could stand on the tip of a pencil.

Hairy monsters

Spiders have hairs on their bodies and on their legs. Some spiders have hairs that are so tiny they are hard to see.

The hairy jumping spider in this picture is shown much bigger than it really is, so you can see its hairs.

When a spider feels its hairs move, it knows that something is moving nearby, even if the spider can't see it.

Spiders taste things through tiny hairs on their front legs.

Some spiders have tufts of special hairs on their feet, which help them to walk up glass.

Under attack

Birds, frogs and lots of other animals eat spiders. Some kinds of spiders even eat other spiders.

Spiders that look like the things around them are hard for attackers to see.

Can you see the spider hiding on this twig?

Some spiders look like sand or tree bark.

Coati

Some tarantulas have hairs that sting.
If they are attacked by an animal like this
coati, they kick their hairs at it.

This spider's bright
markings tell other
animals that it
tastes bad.

Spider tricks

Spiders can do some fantastic tricks.

A few kinds of
spiders can
walk on
water.

The surface of water is like a thin skin.
The spiders have waxy feet. This stops
them from sinking into the water.

Wheel spiders live in hot deserts.

When a wheel spider is attacked, it tucks its legs into its body.

It escapes by rolling away quickly across the hot sand.

Spiky spiders

Some spiders have amazing spikes and spines on their bodies.

Horned spiders have curved spikes on their bodies.
The spikes make it hard for other animals to eat them.

Triangular spiders have spiky front legs which are covered in spiny hairs.

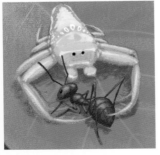

The spider sits very still. It waits until it feels that a bug is near.

The spider's front legs snap closed. It traps the bug and eats it.

29

Glossary of spider words

Here are some of the words in this book you might not know. This page tells you what they mean.

 fangs - the sharp parts of a spider's mouth that it uses to kill things.

 web - a silk net made by a spider. Spiders catch food in their webs.

 silk - the material that a spider uses to make webs and egg sacs.

 egg sac - a silk bag that a spider makes to put her eggs in.

 hatch - to break out of an egg. Baby spiders hatch out of their eggs.

 spiderling - a baby spider. A spiderling looks like a tiny adult spider.

 spine - a thin pointed part of a spider's body or on its legs.

Websites to visit

You can visit some exciting websites to find out more about spiders.

To visit these websites, go to the Usborne Quicklinks Website at **www.usborne-quicklinks.com** Read the internet safety guidelines, and then type the keywords "**beginners spiders**".

The websites are regularly reviewed and the links in Usborne Quicklinks are updated. However, Usborne Publishing is not responsible, and does not accept liability, for the content or availability of any website other than its own. We recommend that children are supervised while on the internet.

Red-kneed tarantulas eat small animals and lizards. After a big meal, they may not eat again for several months.

Index

Acknowledgements

Photographic manipulation by John Russell

Photo credits

The publishers are grateful to the following for permission to reproduce material: © **BBC Natural History Unit Picture Library** (JL Gomez de Francisco) Cover, (Bernard Castelein) 11, (Adrian Davies) 13, (Doug Wechsler) 26, © **Bruce Coleman Collection** (John Cancalosi) 5, (Gordon Langsbury) 10, (Jane Burton) 17, © **Corbis** (Michael Maconachie/Papilio) 2-3, (Joe McDonald) 4, (Layne Kennedy) 6-7, (Kevin Schafer) 9, (Eric and David Hosking) 20-21, (Steve Kaufman) 25, (Lanz Von Horsten/Gallo Images) 27, © **Digital Vision** Title page, 31, © **NHPA** (Stephen Dalton) 8, (GI Bernard) 19, (James Carmichael Jr) 24, (ANT) 29, © **Oxford Scientific Films** (JAL Cooke) 14, (GW Willis) 21, © **Premaphotos Wildlife** (Ken Preston-Mafham) 16, 22-23, 28

First published in 2002 by Usborne Publishing Ltd., Usborne House, 83-85 Saffron Hill, London EC1N 8RT, England. www.usborne.com Copyright © 2007, 2002 Usborne Publishing Ltd. The name Usborne and the devices ♀ ⚭ are Trade Marks of Usborne Publishing Ltd. All rights reserved. No part of this publication may be reproduced, stored in a retrieval system, or transmitted in any form or by any means, electronic, mechanical, photocopying, recording or otherwise without the prior permission of the publisher.
First published in America 2003. U.E. Printed in China.

Sun, moon and stars

Farm animals

Elizabeth I

TRASH AND RECYCLING

Dogs

Horses and ponies

Spiders

Planes

Ancient Greeks

Cats

VOLCANOES

DINOSAURS

Your Body

Armor

Sharks

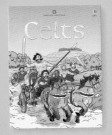
Celts

Vikings

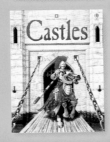
Castles

How flowers grow

Knights

Living in space

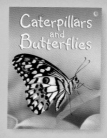
Caterpillars and Butterflies

Ballet

Pirates

Egyptians

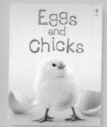
Eggs and Chicks

Romans

Weather

Tadpoles and frogs

Why do we eat?

Under the sea

Bears

Aztecs

TRUCKS

Night Animals

Firefighters

Antarctica

Bugs

COWBOYS

Planet Earth